Cycling

Written in association with
British Cycling

Produced for A & C Black by

Monkey Puzzle Media Ltd
The Rectory, Eyke, Woodbridge
Suffolk IP12 2QW

Published in 2008 by

A & C Black Publishers Ltd
38 Soho Square, London W1D 3HB
www.acblack.com

First edition 2008

ISBN: 978 0 7136 8955 6

Note: While every effort has been made to ensure
that the content of this book is as technically accurate
and as sound as possible, neither the author nor the
publisher can accept responsibility for any injury or
loss sustained as a result of the use of this material.

This book is produced using paper that is made from
wood grown in managed, sustainable forests. It is
natural, renewable and recyclable. The logging and
manufacturing processes conform to the
environmental regulations of the country of origin.

Acknowledgements
Cover and inside design by James Winrow and
Tom Morris for Monkey Puzzle Media Ltd.
Cover photograph of Bradley Wiggins courtesy of
British Cycling.
We would like to thank the following for permission
to reproduce photos: British Cycling pages 4–5, 9
(bottom), 11 (top), 13 (bottom-right), 14–20, 24–28,
30–33, 35–39, 41–42, 44–45, 48–50, 52, 53, 54, 55,
57, 58–59; British Cycling/Joolze Dymond page 12
(top), 43 (bottom); British Cycling/Trek Bikes page 7;
A & C Black/Marshall Thomas pages 6, 8, 9 (top), 12
(bottom), 13 (top and bottom-left), 22–23, 43 (top
row), 46–47; Trek Bikes pages 11 (middle and
bottom), 21, 40; Union Cycliste Internationale/
Daniel Ahlgren Graphics page 34.
Illustration on page 29 reproduced by Dave Saunders
with permission from British Cycling.

The publishers would like to thank John Mills and
Andrew Gillott for their contribution to this book.

KNOW THE GAME is a registered trademark.

Printed and bound in China by C&C Offset Printing
Co., Ltd.

Note: Throughout the book riders and officials are
referred to as 'he'. This should, of course, be taken
to mean 'he or she' where appropriate. Similarly, all
instructions are geared towards right-handed riders –
left-handers should simply reverse these instructions.

CONTENTS

INTRODUCTION

Cycling is a diverse sport. It comes in a variety of forms, and includes leisure activities and competitions. The benefits of taking part in cycling are wide and varied, and cycling's many disciplines offer a number of different health and social benefits to all.

Cycling is a great way of making friends.

CYCLING BENEFITS

Cycling increases people's physical fitness, and the physical aspects of the sport contribute to the development of a healthy lifestyle. But cycling also promotes social skills, through sharing the road or track with others, and emotional wellbeing, by giving people a chance to relax. Cycling is open to almost everyone, whatever their ability or age.

GETTING STARTED

It is not necessary to pick a specific cycling discipline to get started: just getting out and about on a bike can be tremendous fun. Even professional riders often compete in more than one discipline or do something else just for fun – there are, for example, professional road racers who like to relax by going mountain biking (MTB) with their friends. You may find that you are more interested in taking part in one particular discipline however, or your bike may be more suitable to one discipline than another – a BMX bike, for example.

The following pages are an easy guide to understanding your bike and equipment better. Whatever type of bike you have,

Cycling promotes social skills and emotional wellbeing.

and whether you want to ride occasionally for leisure or dream of competing at the highest level, you will be safer and more comfortable if you consider the following advice.

If you have a limited budget, looking for a good second-hand bike is a better option than buying a new, cheap bike.

BIKES

Whatever type of bike you have, it will be safer and more comfortable if it fits you correctly. Frame size is very important, so whenever possible, try to get advice from a local bike shop when choosing a bike. If you are buying second-hand, most manufacturer's websites will give you a good indication of which frame size is best for you, based on your height and inside-leg measurement.

BUYING SECOND-HAND

Buying second-hand is a good idea for the beginner and good quality bikes are manufactured to last for a great many years. A cycling club in your area may well know of second-hand bikes that would be suitable for you, or you could ask a friend who's an experienced cyclist to look at bikes you're interested in and give you some advice.

CLEANING AND MAINTENANCE

As with all equipment, you need to take care of your bike. It is particularly important to clean it regularly – this not only looks better, but it gives you a chance to spot any wear or damage. You should regularly check your bike over, both for safety and to stop any wear and tear getting worse. A reputable bike shop will be able to advise you on, and carry out, any basic repairs that you might require.

BIKE CLEANING

Wash your bike regularly using hot soapy water and a sponge or soft brush.

- Rinse with clean water, taking care not to encourage water into the bearings (hubs, headset, and bottom bracket).
- Either wipe off the excess water or leave it to dry naturally.
- Re-lubricate the chain, gear mechanisms and other moving parts such as the brakes and levers.

PARTS OF A BIKE

All bikes, regardless of their intended purpose, have the same basic components. In cycling there is often a crossover of technology, so components developed for one discipline are now often being used in other disciplines.

 Parts of a bike.

Saddle

Rear sprockets or cassette

Seatpost

Rear derailleur

Brake

Front derailleur

Stem

Headset

Handlebars

Brake lever

Brake

Forks

Tyre

Rim

Crank

Pedal

Chainrings

Chain

Front hub

Spokes

FRAME TYPES

Many types of bike can be adapted for use in a different discipline by simply changing the tyres. For example, changing knobbly tyres on a mountain bike to smooth tyres can adapt it from an off-road machine to a faster road machine.

Frames that can be adapted for different uses include:
• road bikes
• mountain bikes (MTBs)
• cyclo-cross bikes

Specialist frames include those for:
• track bikes
• BMX bikes
• cycle speedway bikes.

Seat tube

Top tube

Seat stay

Fork

Down tube

Chain stay

RIDING POSITION

It is important to get your riding position correct for three reasons.

- Safety – so you can control the bike at all times, especially the brakes.
- Comfort – to enable you to ride for a variety of distances through different terrain and conditions.
- Efficiency – for optimum power output.

SETTING A GENERAL RIDING POSITION

This guide will give you a starting point for good basic riding position.

- While sitting on the bike wearing your usual cycling shoes, put the heel of your foot on the pedal. Ideally, your leg should be straight but not over-stretched when the pedal is at the lowest point. Do this with both legs: some people have one leg slightly shorter than the other, and you need to be guided by the shortest leg!

- Pedal backwards (with heels still on the pedals). Ideally, your hips should not rock from side to side. If they do, lower your saddle a little and try again.

- The saddle needs to be flat for safety and comfort.
- Your weight should be well balanced on your bike, without too much weight on your arms or bottom.
- You should be able to reach and operate the front and back brake levers easily.

BMX riders do not sit on the seat when racing. Their seat is generally set very low, and tilted back for safety during manoeuvres and jumps.

PEDAL POSITION AND ACTION

- Place the ball of your foot on the pedal, above the pedal spindle. Correct foot position allows the maximum amount of power to be transferred to the pedals.
- Place the cranks level and the ball of your foot over the pedal spindle. Ideally, your knee should be over the pedal spindle on the front leg. You can adjust this by altering the saddle setback – sliding the saddle forwards or backwards.
- Pedalling is a circular motion, not just up and down. Practise pedalling with a smooth, continuous (or spinning) action. At the top of the pedal stroke push down and forwards; imagine scraping mud off the sole of your foot at the bottom of the pedal stroke.

The ball of the foot should be directly over the pedal spindle. The centre-line of the foot should be at 90° to the pedal spindle.

The knee of the front foot should be over the pedal spindle.

In downhill (DH), the seat is used more for manoeuvring the bike than for sitting on!

HELMETS, CLOTHING AND FOOTWEAR

Having the right equipment makes cycling safer and a lot more comfortable. This includes helmets, shoes and clothing – and sometimes even body armour!

HELMETS

When cycling, you should wear protective headgear in the form of a hard shell helmet, which in Europe should have a CE mark to show it conforms to European safety and quality standards.

There are two basic types of helmet used in cycling: standard and full-face helmets.

- Standard – the most commonly used helmet in cycling. Standard helmets are lightweight, and provide a good level of head protection in an accident. They are available with vents to help keep your head cool in hot weather or during a tough ride. They also come with different fitting adjustments, to make sure the helmet fits well and does not come off in an accident. Standard helmets are usually used for road riding, cross-country (XC) mountain bike, and cyclo-cross disciplines.

- Full face – this type of helmet is more commonly used in off-road disciplines, such as BMX racing and downhill. It is usually covered with a hard shell, and a chin bar extends out to provide extra protection for the face in case of an accident.

CLOTHING

Cyclists should wear clothing that is comfortable for cycling, taking into consideration any possible changes in the weather. Baggy clothing is not recommended for cycling, as it can get caught in moving parts. Many cyclists choose to wear gloves to protect their palms from being grazed in the event of a fall.

 Body armour and a full-face helmet are essential items of equipment for downhill racers.

 A standard helmet.

A full-face helmet.

CYCLING SHORTS

Cycling shorts are probably the most effective piece of specialist clothing for improving comfort on a bicycle when riding for a reasonable period of time. Cycling shorts are usually made of Lycra and have a synthetic chamois seat pad, which prevents chafing and makes being in the saddle for long periods of time more comfortable. In the specialist disciplines, such as BMX and downhill, many cyclists choose clothing with a looser fit, so that there's room underneath it for body armour.

Looser fit clothing accommodates body armour.

Cycling shorts make being in the saddle more comfortable.

CYCLING SHOES

Trainers or comfortable outdoor shoes are fine if you are cycling once in a while just for fun, though shoelaces need to be safely tucked away or they may get caught in the gears. Most people who cycle more regularly decide to buy a pair of specialist cycling shoes. These have stiff soles made of plastic or carbon fibre, to transfer more power to the pedals, and they use Velcro straps or special ratchet-style fastenings, so that there are no shoelaces to get caught in the chain and moving parts.

A rider's choice of shoe usually depends on what kind of riding they do and the type of pedals on their bike. For example:

- Clipless pedals. These grip on to a cleat attached to the sole of the cycling shoe. To 'clip in', the rider presses down on to the pedal, and to 'clip out', twists the foot sideways. Clipless pedals are used in both on- and off-road disciplines, although off-road pedals are double-sided and designed to shed mud easily. Only specialist shoes can have cleats fitted to them.

- Pedals with toe straps. These are often found on leisure bikes, because they can be used with almost any kind of shoe: wide shoes, though, may not fit in the toe straps. Toe straps are also used by track racers, often as well as clipless pedals, to ensure their feet do not pull out of the pedals.

- Flat pedals. These are used most frequently by BMX, cycle speedway and downhill riders. The pedal platforms usually have pins sticking out of them for extra grip. However, hard soled shoes may not grip the pedals and can slip.

GETTING INVOLVED

Cycling provides excellent opportunities for people of all ages and abilities to take part. Whether you are interested in riding for fun, or want to take your riding more seriously and compete against others, British Cycling has a programme for you.

BRITISH CYCLING

As the internationally recognised governing body of cycling in the UK, British Cycling administers all disciplines of cycling. Its range of responsibilities includes:

- developing the sport, clubs and competition structure, right up to the Great Britain Cycling Team that competes at the World Championships and Olympic Games
- developing leisure cycling in the UK, via the Everyday Cycling programme.

Membership of British Cycling offers a multitude of benefits including access to competitions, insurance cover and British Cycling magazines.

GO-RIDE

Go-Ride is British Cycling's club development programme. It aims to improve opportunities for young riders, and the structure and resources of cycling clubs. Go-Ride focuses on young members and increasing the

 Cycling is for people of all ages and abilities.

number of young riders with access to coaching activities.

There is a national network of Go-Ride cycling clubs, and each has trained British Cycling coaches who run a wide range of cycling activities for under eighteens, ensuring that all abilities are accommodated. The Go-Ride sessions are fun, exciting and challenging for newcomers and more experienced riders alike.

IMPROVING SKILLS

People who want to improve their cycling skills and techniques will find it useful to work with a Go-Ride Club and their cycling coach. Go-Ride coaching activities have been designed to introduce young people to a range of cycling disciplines, such as BMX, cycle speedway, cyclo-cross, mountain biking, road and track riding. So whatever your age or ability, there'll be something to suit your needs.

Go-Ride sessions are fun, exciting and challenging.

Go-Ride will improve skills.

Go-Ride school clubs give pupils a chance to experience cycling. They are also a way for young people to discover whether they are interested in getting involved in competitive cycling.

GO RIDE SESSIONS

Go-Ride sessions teach the necessary skills to make riders more competent cyclists as well as advancing their cycling techniques in a safe, traffic free environment, such as a school playing field or playground. Any type of bike can be used, so long as it is in good condition.

WORKING WITH A COACH

If you are not able to access a Go-Ride club, try finding a British-Cycling-qualified cycling coach. This has benefits for all levels of rider, and some have progressed into competing on the world stage as a member of the GB cycling team.

15

CHOOSING A COACH

When looking for and choosing a coach it is important that you consider a number of factors:

- do they have a valid British Cycling Coaching Licence for the cycling discipline you are interested in?
- do they have a good knowledge of that discipline?

When you contact the coach, be clear on what you want to get out of the coaching relationship: what can they offer and, importantly, what they would require from you?

If you are under 18 years old your parent/guardian should be involved in choosing and working with your coach.

RACING LICENCE

To be able to race in any cycling discipline you must have a racing licence, which is available when you join British Cycling.

GOING RACING

If you want to start racing, the easiest route into competitive cycling is via a Go-Ride club. As well as coaching sessions that will develop race-specific techniques, the club will be able to help with race entries, equipment choice and other advice that will make your first race fun and exciting. For further information on the format of each racing discipline, check the relevant section of this book.

 A coach working with young riders.

GREAT BRITAIN CYCLING TEAM

The Great Britain Cycling Team features a number of development programmes for young riders.

If you have dreams of racing with the world's best cyclists, riding for the Great Britain Cycling Team should be one of your ambitions. Competing in all of the Olympic cycling disciplines (Track, Road, MTB and BMX) the team are one of the most successful in the world, regularly achieving success at the World Championships and Olympic Games.

The Great Britain Cycling Team has developed a series of programmes intended to provide aspiring international cyclists with a smooth development pathway. Many who hope one day to be a champion start along this path between the ages of 14 and 16 years.

BECOMING A COACH

If you are interested in becoming a qualified coach, British Cycling's Coach Education Programme provides the necessary training. The programme consists of four levels of award, starting with coaching basic skills to groups of beginner riders, through to performance coaching for individual riders using the latest coaching and training methods for each of cycling's disciplines.

ROAD RACE AND TIME TRIAL

The two most popular types of competitive cycling are the traditional disciplines of road racing and time trialling. Road riding is a test of stamina, fitness and tactical expertise. Road riders often have particular strengths: cycling uphill very quickly, sprinting in a tight finish, or the ability to race against the clock in individual or team time trials, for example.

ROAD RACING

Most adult road racing takes place on public roads, though there are an increasing number of circuit events on roads closed to other traffic or on specially constructed closed-road cycling circuits. Some circuit racing takes place on shared-use facilities such as motor-racing circuits. All Under-16 racing takes place on traffic-free or closed-road circuits.

TACTICS ON THE ROAD

Road racing is amazingly varied: the tactical options for a rider or team are almost endless. This is what makes it such a wonderful, sometimes unpredictable sport. Often the strongest teams and riders prevail, but the outsider who is prepared to take risks and commit to daring tactics always has a fighting chance.

The first rider over the finish line wins. In the UK, events range from short Youth races of 20km or less, through club-level events of 100km or more, to Elite-level races of more than 200km. Races may be from

Road racing is a test of fitness, stamina and tactical expertise.

ne place to another or be in the form of a circuit race, with the same point for the start and finish, involving one or more laps. A criterium is a multi-lap race on a small circuit, which often takes place in a town centre and is very fast, exciting and spectator-friendly.

STAGE RACES

The bike races known as stage races are contested over several days. Cycling's most prestigious stage races, the 'grand tours' of France, Italy and Spain, last weeks and are among the greatest tests of endurance in modern sport.

- Stage races usually combine various road and time trial events, with each event forming one stage. It is not unusual to have two stages in one day!

- The overall winners are the individual rider and the entire team with the lowest cumulative time at the end of the race.

- There are also prizes for the winner of each stage, the best sprinter and the best climber (known as King or Queen of the Mountains).

The grand tours (ridden by professional cyclists) are gruelling events which test the limits of the human body and mind, with the cyclists riding at very high speeds over huge distances, high mountain passes, and challenging time trial courses.

TOUR DE FRANCE

The most famous of the grand tours is the Tour de France. First held in 1903 over a period of just 6 days, Le Tour in the 21st Century is a huge, three week event, with close to 200 riders fighting for the yellow leader's jersey; Le Maillot Jaune. The average rider burns nearly 130,000 calories in the course of Le Tour – that's the equivalent of 11,000 bananas!

Stage races are amongst the toughest events in modern sport.

TIME TRIALS (TTs)

Many riders who enjoy the thrill of riding individually at high speeds turn to time trialling. If you find you are naturally quick when riding solo and you enjoy pushing the limits of your physical capacity, then time trials may be the discipline for you.

Time trial riders compete individually (or in small teams) against the clock, the course, the conditions and other competitors. The winner is the rider or team who finishes in the fastest time. For many riders, TTs are a personal battle, in which riders continually strive to beat their personal best time.

> TTs are often called the 'races of truth' – because the stopwatch never lies about how well you did!

 Time trials are a personal battle.

TT EVENTS

In the UK, TTs are usually held over standard distances of 10 miles (16km), 25 miles (40km), 50 miles (80km) and 100 miles (160km). There are also longer events such as 12-hour and 24-hour events (where the rider who covers the most distance is the winner).

ROAD AND TIME TRIAL BIKES – SIMILARITIES

Road and time trial bikes incorporate many of the same materials in their construction. Bikes for both disciplines tend to be:

- light (especially road bikes, to make climbing easier)

- aerodynamic (to reduce wind resistance)
- rigid (to reduce power loss and help when sprinting)
- tyres for both disciplines are very narrow and often without tread for added speed, which can make cornering in the rain very difficult!

With light weight and stiffness being major factors, steel has almost been replaced by aluminium, carbon fibre and titanium as the main construction materials for the frames.

ROAD AND TIME TRIAL BIKES – DIFFERENCES

Time trial bikes come in a wide range of shapes and sizes, designed to help the rider become more aerodynamic than when riding any other bike. This is because reduction of wind resistance is extremely important in riding time trials. The main differences of a time trial bike from a road bike are the handlebars and the use of more aerodynamic wheels.

- Drop handlebars are used on a road bike (as in track and cyclo-cross riding) whereas time trial bikes are fitted with aero bars (also known as tri-bars, as they are used in triathlon as well) for increased aerodynamic advantage.
- The use of rear disc wheels and carbon-spoked wheels is allowed in time trials but are not permitted in road races.

 A time trial bike with aero bars, disc wheel and carbon-spoked front wheel.

 A road bike.

KEY TECHNIQUE – CLIMBING

Good climbing ability is essential in road and time trial cycling, particularly in long, hilly road races and hilly time trials. Climbing combines all of the techniques of efficient pedalling and gear selection with other techniques and skills, such as balance and coordination.

Climbs can be ridden either in or out of the saddle. In terms of energy use, it is more efficient to ride in the saddle, so on a long climb it is better to stay seated most or all of the time. But more force can be harnessed when riding out of the saddle; on short, steep climbs, as a way of establishing a gap between yourself and other riders, or as a way of closing a gap, standing on the pedals can be very useful.

The essential components of climbing are:

- riding at a comfortable cadence (cadence is the number of pedal revolutions per minute)
- careful gear selection
- keeping a good pedalling rhythm
- effective cornering (especially on very steep sections)
- correct body position.

Correct body position is dependent on how steep a slope you are riding up. You need to move your weight forward as your centre of gravity changes, dependent on whether you are in or out of the saddle. The steeper the slope, the further forward you need to shift your weight.

On a long climb it is better to stay seated most or all of the time.

In order to climb effectively you will need to:

- assess the length, gradient and surface conditions
- select a low gear that is easy to pedal
- keep your head up, ride in as straight a line as possible, look as far ahead as possible and watch for changes in the slope ahead, so that you can be ready to shift gears if required.

Do not apply brakes, except when an urgent stop is needed or when approaching an obstacle, as this will significantly reduce your momentum.

When climbing in the saddle:

- position hands on the outside of the tops of the handlebars
- move weight towards the back of the bike
- sit upright and relaxed to aid breathing.

When climbing out of the saddle:

- position hands on the tops of the brakes or on the tops of the handlebars
- move weight towards the front of the bike
- keep the bike moving in a straight line.

On short, steep climbs, standing on the pedals can be a useful technique.

TRACK

Track cycling is an exciting discipline for both spectators and riders, encompassing showmanship, tactics and extreme physical performance. The two main categories of event are Sprint and Endurance.

TYPES OF RIDER

The physical differences between sprint and endurance riders are huge, track endurance riders generally being thin and able to ride for hours, while track sprinters are muscular and able to ride at high speeds for short periods.

ONE-HOUR RECORD

The world one-hour record is held by Chris Boardman. Boardman covered 49.441km at the Manchester Velodrome on 27 October 2000: an average speed of just over 30 mph.

 A track endurance rider.

 A track sprinter.

EVENTS

There are many regional and national variations of track events, which makes track riding dynamic and versatile. Most of these variations are based around the main World Championship and Olympic events.

SPRINT EVENTS

There are individual and team sprint events over a variety of distances:

Kilometre Time Trial (Kilo)
A time trial against the clock, ridden from a standing start. No qualifying rounds make this a high-pressure, one-chance event. The kilometre is only ridden by junior and senior men.

500m Time Trial
As above but half the distance, ridden by junior and senior women, and both male and female under 16s.

Team Sprint

Three-man or two-women teams ride three laps of the track (men) or two laps for women (on Olympic standard 250m tracks). A rider peels off after their lap is completed and plays no further part in the race, leaving the next rider to complete the next or final lap. This is technically demanding because the second and third riders slipstream (ride closely behind) the leading rider, saving up to 30 per cent of energy and leaving them relatively fresh for their turn. The team sprint is usually ridden by two teams at a time, which start on opposite sides of the track. There is a qualifying round, with the four fastest winning teams going through to the finals for gold, silver and bronze.

The Women's Team Sprint.

SPRINT EVENTS (CONT.)

Keirin

The Keirin (Japanese for 'fight') is a race in which riders sprint for the line after completing a series of laps behind a single motorbike pacer (called a derny). The derny gradually builds up speed, with riders jockeying for position behind (they must not pass the derny until it peels off the track). The derny pulls on to the track centre with two and a half laps to go and from then on it's a race for the line. Tactical and often very physical, it's a great spectator event.

Match Sprint

The match sprint is a simple head-to-head sprint between two riders, over three laps of the track. At the highest level there is usually a qualifying 200m flying start time trial to organise the seeding. From then on there are a series of knockout rounds leading to quarter-finals, semis and the final. These latter rounds are usually ridden on a best-of-three basis.

> **A track sprinter at full speed can produce over 2,200 watts of power – enough to power 25 light bulbs or 554 personal music players!**

 The Keirin.

ENDURANCE EVENTS

As with the sprints, the variety of distances and types of race make distance cycling on a track a varied and exciting activity.

Individual Pursuit

This is the ultimate head-to-head endurance race. Pairs of riders begin from a standing start on opposite sides of the track. They literally pursue each other for 4,000m (3,000m for women). There is usually a qualifying round from which the fastest riders progress to a second round, where the top riders compete for places in the gold and silver, and bronze finals. In the finals, the fastest rider wins, unless one rider is caught by the other, at which point the race is over.

Team Pursuit

This is the team version of the individual pursuit. The big difference from the individual is that the four men, or three women, share the workload, with the lead rider staying at the front for a lap or so before swinging up the track (to the right) and re-joining the line at the back. The Team Pursuit is a technical event, where team-mates often ride only centimetres apart to maximise slipstreaming effects. Times are taken when the third member of the team crosses the line. In the male Team Pursuit, the slowest rider often sacrifices himself in the later stages of the event, riding up the banking and stopping racing so that his team-mates can complete the race without him.

 The Team Pursuit.

ENDURANCE EVENTS (CONT.)

Points Race
This is a bunch race with 20 to 30 riders competing over 20, 30 or 40km. Riders aim to gain points, with the highest score winning the event. Points can be scored at 'intermediate' sprints, often every 10, 20 or 25 laps. Points can also be scored by lapping the field. This is a very tactical event, with alliances being formed and broken and dramatic attacks being chased down by the field. The race requires speed, stamina, the ability to sprint quickly to collect points, and a cool head.

Madison
A male-only event that is effectively a points race for two-man teams. Only one rider per pairing is ever actually racing. The other rider circles the track high up the banking waiting to be caught by his team-mate, at which point he swoops down and his team-mate transfers his momentum using a hand-sling – a combined handshake and slinging motion. The other rider then takes over the racing for the pair. The Madison is highly technical and very exciting to watch. Again, the winner is the team with the most points.

Scratch Race
This is a simple bunch race usually held over 10, 15, 20 or 25km, with the first over the line being the winner. Riders with endurance but poor sprinting abilities may favour the tactic of lapping the field to avoid a final sprint whilst riders with a powerful sprint will favour saving their efforts to the very end.

 Performing the Madison handsling.

TRACK VENUES – INDOOR TRACKS

Normally 250m in length (but sometimes shorter), indoor tracks can have banking as steep as 60 degrees. They are usually made of wood: Britain's three indoor tracks – the National Cycling Centre in Manchester, the Wales National Velodrome in Newport and the velodrome at the Calshot Activities Centre – are all made of Siberian pine

TRACK VENUES – OUTDOOR TRACKS

Outdoor tracks can often be as long as 500m and are most commonly made of asphalt or concrete. They are often found in public parks or as part of a multi-use facility such as the border surrounding a running track.

OUTDOOR GRASS TRACK

A grass track can be marked up on any suitable grass area, such as a sports field, park or a running track and is an ideal discipline for a school environment. Any area that is reasonably flat and even, of a suitable size and free of potential hazards can be easily converted into a grass track for the day. There is no fixed length for a grass track, although they are normally 250–400m and typically have 47–55m straights and a finish line midway along one side. The size is often determined by the venue, particularly if the track has to follow the outside of another facility, such as a running track.

Track Diagram

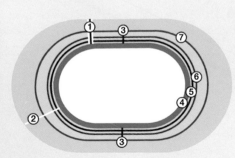

①	Finish line
②	200m line
③	Pursuit start and finish lines
④	Côte d'Azur
⑤	Datum line
⑥	Sprinters line
⑦	Stayers line

A typical 250m indoor track layout.

KEY TECHNIQUE – RIDING A FIXED-WHEEL BIKE

A track bike has no brakes and a single, fixed gear – the pedals are directly connected to the rear wheel. This means that if you stop pedalling, the bike will stop moving. To pedal a fixed-wheel bicycle correctly, you should:

- control your speed by steadily decreasing or increasing the pressure on the pedals
- pedal in circles by applying an even pressure throughout the pedal stroke
- keep a constant leg speed, or cadence
- keep your head up and look where you are going!
- keep your upper body relaxed
- not try to stop suddenly, but slow down gradually.

TRACK EQUIPMENT

All riders on a track session should make sure they have two main pieces of safety equipment: a standard cycling helmet without a peak or face mask; and a thin pair of gloves, which protect their hands in a fall and allow them to grip the bars.

CLOTHING

Newcomers to track cycling will rarely have special clothing, but other clothes can be used without any problems if the general guidelines earlier in this book are followed. Clothing for track cycling needs to allow for a full range of movement without being too loose or baggy.

BIKES

Track bikes are relatively simple, without gears and brakes. With bikes having a fixed wheel (forcing you to pedal continuously) the rider controls speed through pressure applied to the pedals. Bikes fall into two broad categories.

Upright bikes
These have conventional dropped handlebars and traditional spoked or carbon-spoked wheels. These bikes are used for bunch endurance races and sprint events like the Keirin and match sprint.

Low-profile bikes
These have extended aero bars for a more aerodynamic position. Wheels are often carbon spoked or carbon disc. Handling and manoeuvrability are sacrificed for aerodynamic efficiency. These bikes are used for endurance events like pursuit races and sprint events like the Kilo and 500m TT.

 An upright track bike.

 A low-profile track bike.

BMX

Bicycle moto-cross (BMX) is an extremely exciting discipline that is great fun for all of the family. Up to eight riders race around a 300–450m track that has jumps, bumps and berms (banked corners). Racing takes place indoors and outdoors, with each race lasting between 30 and 40 seconds. Some riders reach speeds over 30 mph (48 kph).

 BMX is the newest Olympic disipline.

BMX racing is the newest Olympic cycling discipline, making its first appearance at the 2008 Games in Beijing.

BMX RACING

Once the riders leave the start gate, it is a case of maintaining as much speed as possible. Modern technical tracks allow for only a few short periods of approximately 2–4 seconds in a race when riders can pedal. It is important that riders develop their skills so that speed is not lost through obstacles. This requires mastering pumping, manualling and jumping smoothly. The start is extremely important in BMX racing, a race can be won or lost in the first pedal revolutions– strength, power, technique and mental toughness are crucial.

BMX EVENTS – RACE MEETINGS

A race meeting, be it international, national, regional or club will follow the same basic format.

Motos
Motos are single-lap, qualifying races. Each rider rides three motos and the most successful proceed to the next round.

Qualifying rounds – these are knockout rounds, including quarter-finals and semi-finals and the first four riders in a category qualify to the next round.

Final – a meeting finishes with a final of eight riders.

Championships
In the UK, along with the British National BMX Championships and National Series, a number of regions organise their own regional championships.

International
The majority of BMX riders can compete in most international competitions. National squads are chosen to compete in the UCI BMX Supercross World Cup Series, the European and UCI World BMX Championships, and the Olympic Games.

BMX JARGON

- Bunny hop – lifting both wheels off the ground simultaneously to clear an obstacle.
- Manual (or manualling) – performing a wheelie without pedalling.
- Pumping – using a pumping motion to lift and push down on or off a jump, to gain more speed.
- Wheelie – lifting the front wheel off the ground and holding it there by pedalling.

Strength, power and technique are essential to BMX racing.

THE BMX TRACK

BMX racing takes place on a huge variety of exciting and challenging tracks. The general traits of a BMX track include:

- 300–450m in length
- a raised start hill
- a start gate at the top of the start hill that can accommodate up to eight riders
- at least three banked turns (known as berms)
- a number of obstacles for the riders to negotiate – speed jumps, doubles, table tops and rhythm sections are just some of the names given to these challenges

- the berms are banked to help the riders maintain speed when cornering.

BMX BIKES AND EQUIPMENT

Standard BMX wheels are 20 inches in diameter. Some bikes have 24-inch wheels – these are called cruiser bikes, and are ridden in their own class. Frame materials tend to be alloys of steel, aluminium or titanium, although carbon fibre is now becoming more common in BMX bike construction.

 An Olympic BMX track layout.

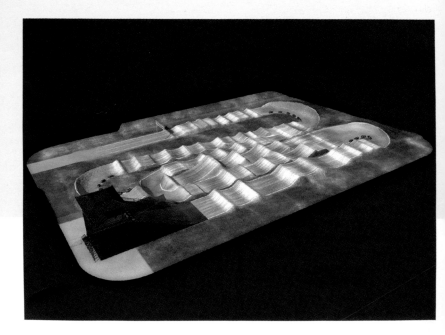

most people will be familiar with a BMX bike. Race-type BMX bikes, however, tend to differ from the usual street variety. They have only a rear brake, no accessories such as foot pegs on the axles, and the frame angles are less steep than the street-type bike.

BMX CLOTHING AND PROTECTION

BMX clothing is heavily influenced by motocross (an off-road motorcycle sport) and is designed for protection:

Head
Helmets are compulsory, and are designed to provide protection both from crashes and flying rocks and dirt. They are much stronger than for most other cycling disciplines, and extend to cover the ears. BMX helmets can be full-face (snug-fitting with mouth guard) or open, but must cover a rider's ears. Full-face moto-cross style helmets are very common.

Hands
Full-fingered gloves are used for protection and grip.

Upper body
Loose fitting long-sleeved shirts are common and practical, providing room for body armour to be worn underneath.

Lower body
Riders wear ankle-length bottoms, which can range from a tracksuit to full motocross-style race kit. Trousers are padded to provide protection from crashes and tend to be baggy to provide room for shin and knee protectors.

Full body
Many riders use additional protective equipment, including leg and arm protectors and various types of body armour. Protection is generally comprised of articulated elbow and kneepads, usually made of plastic with a foam lining.

Footwear and pedals
Clipless pedal and shoe systems are allowed at senior level in Britain, but most riders use flat-sole trainers and flat pedals.

 BMX clothing is designed for protection.

MOUNTAIN BIKE RACING

Mountain biking is a relatively young discipline; it started in the USA in the early 1980s, with a few riders making their own bikes. Today, mountain bikes make up two thirds of all bikes sold in the UK. Many are used for leisure rather than racing, but the two most popular kinds of mountain bike racing are cross-country and downhill.

GETTING STARTED

Getting started in mountain biking is often simply a case of getting a basic mountain bike and going out and exploring the local countryside. Bicycles can legally use bridle paths and the UK has a superb network of these – learn to read a map and get out and enjoy yourself! The pleasure of riding in a traffic-free environment cannot be understated and every ride has the potential to become a mini adventure.

CROSS-COUNTRY (XC) RACING

Endurance, fitness and bike control all combine to make a top XC rider. Riders usually compete on a five- to seven-mile course with climbing, descending, single-track and technical sections (e.g. tight turns, rocks, mud, and banks). Less experienced riders enter a different category (usually 'sport' or 'fun' for newcomers) and complete fewer laps.

▶ Endurance, fitness and bike control make a top XC rider.

Racers all start at the same time and compete on a marked lap. Elite-level riders race for up to two and a half hours, and an even longer 'marathon' category made its debut at the 2003 World Championships – marathons can be 50km, 100km or even 150km in length.

ENDURO RACING

As well as hard-core XC and marathon racing, there has been a huge growth in enduro racing in recent years. Enduros come in many forms – 12- and 24-hour races are just two of the popular options, often with two and four-person teams. Huge fields make for a great atmosphere and, whilst the more able riders treat them as seriously as any other race, for many they are a chance to enjoy riding in company or have a weekend away with friends.

A puncture or mechanical failure during an XC event can put you out of the race, no matter how fast you are. Regularly practising repairing punctures or putting your chain back on can save you vital seconds in a race.

XC MOUNTAIN BIKING

Cross-country mountain bike racing is one of the newest forms of cyclesport.

- In 1990, mountain bike racing was recognised by the UCI and the first official World Championships were held.
- The sport became part of the Olympics in 1996 and the Commonwealth Games in 2002.

Enduro events are an opportunity to challenge yourself within a great atmosphere.

DOWNHILL

Many riders who enjoy the thrill of technically challenging mountain biking turn to downhill. If you find you're naturally quick through technical terrain and you enjoy learning about the limits of handling off-road, then this may be the discipline for you. But good skill levels alone won't do: the races are short, but they require high levels of fitness, especially strength and speed.

DOWNHILL COURSES

Downhill races are marked tracks down which riders race individually, against the clock. The one with the fastest time wins. The riders test their skill and nerve against a challenging succession of jumps, bumps, berms (cambered corners) and drop-offs on a course which is predominantly downhill – often dropping between 300 and 600m in perhaps 2.5km of racing! The course usually takes between 2 and 5 minutes to get down.

TRAIL CENTRES

There are a growing number of purpose-built venues (usually called trail centres) for mountain-biking

Downhill is fast, technical and thrilling.

throughout the UK. These cater for riders of all abilities, and offer a huge network of fun and challenging trails. Trail centres often have extra facilities to make your day there more enjoyable, and it's common to find a café, bike wash, shops and showers.

Some trail centres have become legendary in mountain bike circles: Coed-Y-Brenin in North Wales, Afan Forest Park in South Wales (www.mbwales.com), and Glentress in the Scottish Borders (which is part of the very successful 7 Stanes Mountain Bike Trails network: www.7stanes.gov.uk). Up-to-date information on mountain-bike facilities and venues is also available from the British Cycling website www.britishcycling.org.uk.

GRADED TRAILS

Mountain bike trails are often colour coded or graded by level of difficulty, much like ski runs. Green trails are usually suitable

TAKING THE RIGHT TRAIL

Before attempting to ride any trail, regardless of colour grade, you should check with the trail centre that it is suitable to your ability.

- Green – beginners and novice riders
- Blue – basic off-road skills required
- Red – intermediate
- Black – expert only

for beginners; for blue trails you will need basic off-road skills, such as being able to descend confidently and brake safely on loose surfaces. Red trails are for proficient mountain bike riders only, and black trails are only suitable for expert riders.

Downhill racing at Fort William, Scotland.

MOUNTAIN BIKES

Many riders start mountain biking with a general-purpose bike. Normally this is a 'hardtail' – a bike with suspension forks on the front and no suspension at the back. More experienced riders sometimes later decide to get a bike that is more suited to the kind of riding they enjoy most:

Cross-country (XC) mountain bikes

These are extremely light and often very technically advanced. For cross-country MTBs, carbon fibre, titanium and aluminium are the most popular frame materials. Frames are smaller than those of road bikes, to allow easy dismounting off-road and to aid strength. Longer seat posts compensate for this. Tyres are light and knobbly, and a variety of tread patterns is available for different riding conditions.

XC bikes normally have suspension forks to make the ride more comfortable. In recent years there has been a move towards full suspension bikes (with suspension both front and back) for XC riding. For some courses and conditions, though, a hardtail is still favoured by many riders.

Downhill bikes

With gravity helping the rider to keep the bike up to speed, light weight is not as important in a downhill mountain bike. The key things are strength, handling and suspension. Downhill bikes are highly specialised, with several inches of suspension travel front and rear. Tyres are very broad and heavily knobbled. Transmission consists of only a single front sprocket, and the chain has guides to help keep it in place through the heavy knocks and vibration of competition. Brakes are very powerful discs, and the geometry is set up to provide straight-line stability.

A full-suspension mountain bike.

A hardtail mountain bike.

XC – HARDTAIL v FULL SUSPENSION

Almost all mountain bike racers use at least front suspension forks. The weight of these fell dramatically with the use of carbon fibre, and there are suspension forks that do not weigh much more than rigid forks. Most XC racers use a hardtail bike, which tends to be lighter and stiffer than a full suspension bike and therefore better for climbing and acceleration.

Full suspension bikes are great on flatter, bumpier courses, where the suspension travel at the rear allows the rider to pedal harder through rough sections than a hardtail bike. Both front and rear suspension can be locked out when required, to allow faster climbing.

TYRE TALK

The type, condition and inflation pressure of tyres affects their grip on the ground.

- Tyres inflated to higher pressure have less grip, but more speed.
- Tyres inflated to lower pressure offer more grip as there is more surface area in contact with the ground, but may roll more slowly as a result.

 Downhill bikes are designed to tackle extreme terrain.

DESCENDING

Descending skills are important for both safety and speed. Poor descending skills can result in considerable loss of time and can also increase the risk of an accident. Descending combines all the skills of braking and cornering, alongside other techniques and skills, such as choosing the right line through a corner and making the right gear selection.

The essential components of descending are: observation and anticipation of changes in direction, terrain or conditions, good braking technique, effective cornering, and proper gear selection. Correct body position is dependent on the severity of the gradient. Riders need to move their weight back as their centre of gravity changes due to the gradient of the slope. The steeper the slope, the further back they need to shift their weight.

Descending skills are important for both safety and speed.

KEY TECHNIQUE – DESCENDING

In order to descend effectively you will need to:

- Assess the length, gradient, visibility and surface conditions.
- Select a high (hard) gear.
- Position hands over the brakes, while moving weight back over the saddle.
- Keep feet level with each other to maintain balance.
- Control speed by applying mostly the rear brake, with a little front brake. Try not to skid – if you do, slowly release and then reapply the brakes.
- Keep your head up, looking for obstructions on the trail ahead.

Fast, confident descending is an essential element of competitive mountain bike racing.

CYCLO-CROSS

Cyclo-cross is the original off-road cycling discipline, becoming popular in Europe during the 1940s and 1950s – long before the mountain bike arrived on the scene!

WINTER TRAINING

Cyclo-cross, which is often referred to as just 'cross', was originally developed to offer a fun winter training pastime for road riders. It therefore has its competitive season through the autumn and winter months, and is popular today with both road riders and mountain bike riders, helping them to maintain fitness during their off-season. It is often seen as a safe and fun alternative to long road rides in cold winter weather.

A HARD BATTLE

Cyclo-cross is a very exciting branch of cycling with action-packed racing, which is great for riders and spectators alike. It is also one of the most accessible and welcoming forms of cycling. Cross races have a relaxed, informal atmosphere, and you can normally enter local races on the day. Better riders quickly lap slower competitors, but that is not the end of the race – riders can still enjoy their own private battles, whether they are first or 101st. Mountain bikes are welcome at most British cyclo-cross races.

Cyclo-cross is the original off-road discipline.

> Cyclo-cross races often have categories for younger riders, who ride for less time and usually pay a reduced entry fee.

The Three Peaks, staged in the Yorkshire Dales National Park, is the UK's most famous and enduring cyclo-cross race.

- The first race took place in 1961.
- Riders race over the three peaks of Ingleborough (723m), Whernside (736m) and Pen-Y-Ghent (694m).
- The Three Peaks is a tough event – 61km in total, with 1524m of climbing!

CYCLO-CROSS EVENTS

Cyclo-cross races take place in a variety of venues, including town parks, local woods and school or open fields. The venues are usually grassy but often contain a variety of other surfaces such as mud, sand, tarmac and sometimes snow and patches of ice.

Cyclo-cross courses are shorter than mountain bike courses (typically less than 2km per lap) and generally less technically demanding, but often require riders to dismount to clear obstacles – usually artificial ones placed on the circuit by organisers. These typically include wooden boards (about 40cm high), as well as natural obstacles, such as stream or ditch crossings. The race format is very simple – all the riders start together and the first rider across the line after one hour of racing wins. Races for younger riders can be as short as 10–15 minutes.

▶ Riders are often required to dismount for obstacles.

CYCLO-CROSS BIKES

At first glance, cyclo-cross bikes look very similar to a typical road bike, but closer inspection highlights a number of differences.

- Cyclo-cross frames are generally slightly smaller for a given rider than road frames. This makes them stiffer and stronger, and aids mounting and dismounting.

- Saving weight is more important than an aerodynamic riding position. Even so, fatter (and therefore heavier) tyres are used with a knobbly tread pattern similar to mountain bike tyres.

- Pedals are the same double-sided clipless pedals as used on mountain bikes, which enable riders to engage their pedals quickly whilst riding over rough ground. The design of these pedals also prevents them getting clogged-up with mud.

- Cross riders also use mountain-bike style shoes with grippy soles and recessed cleats, which allow them to run when they dismount the bike.

- Cyclo-cross riders use lower (easier) gears than on the road, because riding through dirt and mud, and up and down steep slopes, makes it harder to ride at high speed.

Fast dismount technique.
1. Swing your right leg behind the saddle.
2. Bring the right leg forward between the bike and your left leg.
3. Put your right foot down and then your left so you are jogging with your bike.

Fast mount technique.
1. Run alongside the bike with both hands on the handlebars.
2. Jump onto the saddle, landing on the inside of the thigh.
3. Let your feet find the pedals and start pedalling.

KEY TECHNIQUE – FAST DISMOUNT

Cyclo-cross courses feature obstacles and steep banks; mounting and dismounting quickly are important techniques in cyclo-cross racing.

To learn to dismount quickly, you should:
• Begin at a slow speed that you are comfortable with and use your brakes to slow down if necessary. You can build up speed as you become more proficient.
• Keep both hands on the handlebars.
• Swing your right leg behind the saddle and bring it between the bike and your left leg.
• Put your right foot down on the ground and take your left leg off the pedal so you are jogging with the bike.
• You can progress to a running dismount or try dismounting with your left leg first.

To mount quickly, you should:
• Run alongside your bike with both hands on the handlebars.
• Jump onto the saddle landing on the inside of your thigh.
• Let your feet find the pedals and start pedalling before you run out of speed.

Aim to go straight from the run into jumping on in one smooth motion. You can start by practising this slowly or walking alongside the bike instead of running.

CYCLE SPEEDWAY

Cycle speedway developed in the late 1940s. Riders hurtle around a short oval track. Racers go anti-clockwise from a standing start. Many of the tracks, which vary in length from 60 to 90m, are situated in public parks, sports complexes and recreation centres.

SPEEDWAY SKILLS

Speedway involves clever starting, cornering and passing skills. The rounds happen quickly, one after the other, and riders sometimes need to be ready to compete again in just a few minutes. The racing is exciting for competitors and spectators alike. The close races and tight circuits make it ideal for spectators.

CYCLE SPEEDWAY BIKES AND EQUIPMENT

Cycle speedway bikes are simple and tough, and are designed to accelerate quickly and corner well. The bikes have wider handlebars and an upright riding position for good cornering. The handlebars on a cycle speedway bike are unique in design: upright and heavily swept back.

Slick, treadless tyres are used for indoor racing. For the outdoor season special tyres are used, which have a knobbly tread pattern similar to cyclo-cross tyres but not as extreme as MTB tyres. These help grip to the loose surfaces. Bikes have no brakes and only one gear (a small one to enable riders to accelerate quickly). Unlike track bikes, speedway bikes do not have a freehub.

To improve the grip between the shoes and pedals, cycle speedway riders often glue very coarse sand paper to their pedals. This means that they can get even more grip to help them with the hard initial acceleration from the starting line.

 Sandpaper on pedals helps with grip.

KEY TECHNIQUE – CORNERING

Success in cycle speedway racing requires excellent cornering ability. The circuits are often loose surfaced, so riders must feel comfortable allowing the bike to slide from time to time. Due to the high speed and tight bends, speedway bikes need to lean or bank over a long way.

As with cornering on any bike, it is important to keep your centre of gravity over the wheels, and keep your eyes parallel with the horizon and focused toward the exit of the bend.

In order to corner effectively you will need to:

- Avoid clipping the ground with the pedals; the outside leg should be straight and the inside pedal should be up.
- Put weight on the outside pedal by pushing down with your outside foot. This helps to keep the weight over the wheels and provides traction.
- Additional balance and control may be gained by lifting the inside leg off the pedal and holding it out forward or to the side. This helps with balancing the bike as it leans over, and also means you can put your foot down quickly if necessary.

EVERYDAY CYCLING

There are over two million bicycles sold in the UK every year. Some are raced in the many different forms of cyclesport; however, the vast majority are used for leisure (non-competitive) cycling of one kind or another. Here are a few of the activities in which Britain's leisure cyclists participate.

COMMUTING

Thousands of people ride their bikes to work every day.

Commuting by bike is a healthier, cheaper and often faster alternative to driving or public transport and it's better for the environment too.

In order to increase your safety and confidence on the roads, you should also take part in National Standard Cycle Training. For details of National Standard Cycle Training schemes in your area visit www.britishcycling.org.uk.

TOURING AND TRAIL RIDING

Touring is the cycling equivalent of hiking, often for several days, using a road or mountain bike and carrying your gear with you. There are safe and clearly marked cycle routes both on and off-road. Local tourist information centres have detailed maps and information. If you want to explore an area of countryside you can simply buy a map and make use of the extensive network of cycle routes, off-road trails, bridle paths and rights-of-way throughout the UK.

AUDAX AND CYCLO-SPORTIF

Audax events are long-distance organised rides where the aim is to tackle set distances (usually 100, 200 or 300km) within a certain time period. Similar in nature, but more closely allied to road racing, are Cyclo-Sportif rides. Although not races, these events often take place over the same routes as road races and many riders tackle these events for the sense of achievement it gives them.

BIKEABILITY

Bikeability is the new National Standard for cycle training, designed to give cyclists the skills to ride on today's roads.

Bridle paths, unlike footpaths, are legal rights of way for cyclists. Never ride on footpaths.

Bikes are great for exploring the countryside.

Charity cycle rides are an opportunity to challenge yourself and raise money.

CHARITY CYCLE RIDES

Charity cycle rides are an excellent way to ride a set distance without the pressures of racing. These are often very well organised events. Riders enjoy the opportunity of achieving a certain distance or time, as well as the satisfaction of raising money for charity. Many people also find that charity rides are a great way to make new friends and explore an interesting area.

EVERYDAY CYCLING

The Everyday Cycling website (www.everydaycycling.com) is designed to help people get the most out of their cycling. There are some great features to motivate people to ride further and more often, including news, event details, and routes and rides. Whether it is trips to work or mountain-bike epics, you can choose a challenge to suit your lungs and legs. You can record everything from a quick spin to the paper shop, to the challenge of cycling from Lands End to John O' Groats in your personal Activity Log, chat about bikes till you're blue in the face, set group challenges, and be a part of the Everyday Cycling online community.

The whole family will enjoy the
challenge of Cyclo-Sportif.

DISABILITY CYCLING

Cycling became a Paralympic sport in Seoul in 1988, and is now practised in more than 40 countries. The competition programme includes road and track events, with riders grouped together according to their disability. The main cycling events include the Paralympic Games, World Championships, European Championships, World Cups and the National Championships.

DISABILITY CATEGORIES

A visually impaired rider and a sighted pilot.

Disability cycling can be divided into several categories, as follows.

Visual Impairment
There are various types of visual impairment (VI), ranging from total blindness to a visual field of less than 20 degrees, which is classed as legally blind. (A legally blind individual would have to stand 6m from an object to see it as clearly as a sighted person could from 60m). VI Paralympic events include track (sprint, kilometre and pursuit), road race and time trial.

Cerebral Palsy

Cerebral palsy (CP) is a condition that interferes with the normal development of the brain. People with CP have limited ability to move, and to maintain balance and posture. A brain injury acquired later in life can also result in symptoms of CP. For cycling competitions, riders either compete on bicycles or tricycles. CP Paralympic events include track, road race and time trial.

Locomotor

Individuals with locomotor (LC) disabilities may have had an amputation, a decrease in muscle strength or function, motor paralysis of limbs, shortening of limbs or some other limb dysfunction present from birth. Riders' bikes can be adapted to suit them: for example, handlebar adaptations are allowed for riders with upper-limb disabilities.

LC Paralympic events include track (1km for men, 500m for women, and pursuit), plus the road race and time trial. Additionally there is a team sprint on the track, combining the locomotor and cerebral palsy categories.

Disability road and track events take place in over 40 countries.

DISABILITY CATEGORIES (CONT.)

Learning Disability

A learning disability (LD) is a condition in which the brain does not develop as fast or as fully as it should. LD riders may compete on bicycles, tricycles and tandems, depending on the severity of their disability.

LD riders can compete in the Special Olympics, where the events range from 500m time trials to 40km road races.

Handcycling

With the exception of the Visual Impairment category, all of the disability categories can compete on handcycles. (Separate handcycle competitions are also open to those without a disability.) Paralympic events for handcyclists include road race and time trial.

Handcycles are propelled with the arms, shoulders, chest, back, and/or torso, depending on the level and nature of the disability. Handcycling is mainly for riders who normally require a wheelchair for general mobility, or riders not able to use a conventional bicycle or tricycle because of a severe lower-limb disability.

There are two basic forms of handcycle: one simply attaches to a wheelchair and is generally used for recreational purposes; the other is a stand-alone recumbent tricycle, in which the rider controls the cycle from a laid-back position. This is the machine used for competitive handcycling.

Paralympic handcycling events include road race and time trial.

DRUG-FREE SPORT

For almost as long as there has been competition, individuals have looked for extra advantages that will help them beat their rivals. Advances in equipment, training and coaching can all lead to honest improvements in performance. Unfortunately, there are also people who turn to the dishonest, illegal use of drugs.

COMPETITIVE PRESSURES

There are many reasons why people use drugs, but frequently it is because of their strong desire to win, and the pressure that may be placed on them to win. The rewards of winning, such as fame, fortune and admiration from others, may convince some people that taking drugs is worth the associated risks. However, using drugs is cheating, and means that you have not competed fairly against other competitors.

HEALTH IMPLICATIONS

The use of drugs to gain an advantage when competing can have considerable consequences upon a person's health and can cause irreversible damage. Some drugs are so addictive and harmful that they are not just banned in sport – they are illegal to use or have in your possession.

CATCHING UP WITH THE CHEATS

Those who compete in sport have to undergo regular drug testing. Increases in technology mean that catching those who use drugs is now easier than ever: the tests become more sophisticated every year, and an increasing number of drug cheats are now being caught.

MEDICATION AND SUPPLEMENTS

If you are competing in sport, you have to be very careful about what medication and supplements you use, because they may contain substances that are banned. The '100% ME' website (www.100percentme.co.uk) will provide you with further information on the use of drugs in sport, and also links to a central database where medicines can be checked for banned substances. The '100% ME' programme has been created to increase the awareness and understanding of drug-free sport, underlining the fact that if you have the right attitude, determination and focus, you can achieve great success without taking drugs.

> **If you have ever cheered on your favourite rider to victory, imagine how meaningless that victory would be if you discovered they had used drugs to succeed.**

◀ 100% ME ambassadors help to increase understanding of drug-free sport.

▶ If you have the right attitude, determination and focus you can do it on your own without the need for taking drugs

GLOSSARY

100% ME Education and information programme promoting drug-free sport, and the positive attitudes and values of sportsmen and women in the UK who have competed successfully in sport.

Audax Long-distance bike ride, often mass participation. Traditional audax events have timed stages.

BMX Bicycle motocross. Fast and furious racing over jumps, bumps and obstacles on 20-in and 24-in wheeled bikes.

Body armour Collective term for protective clothing worn on the arms, legs and body. Body armour is worn by BMX, mountain bike and cycle speedway riders.

British Cycling Internationally recognised governing body of cyclesport in the UK.

Chamois Padded, shaped insert in cycling shorts, now made from synthetic material but historically made of leather.

Cleat Metal component that fits to the bottom of a cycling shoe and interfaces with a clipless pedal.

Clipless pedal Pedal designed to interface with a cleat, attaching the rider to the pedals without the need for toe-clips.

Cruiser BMX BMX with 24-inch wheels.

Cycling Ireland Internationally recognised governing body of cyclesport in Ireland.

CX Commonly used abbreviation for cyclo-cross.

Derailleur Moveable chain guide operated by a lever or shifter which is usually mounted on the handlebars. Bikes with multiple gears normally have a front and rear derailleur.

DH Commonly used abbreviation for downhill mountain biking.

Downhill Commonly used abbreviation for downhill mountain biking.

Enduro Long-distance, mass participation off-road event. Although some are timed, enduros are often sociable and non-competitive events.

Everyday Cycling British Cycling's non-competitive programme, which encourages participation and enjoyment of cycling in all its forms.

Fixed-wheel Bicycle without a freehub and with just one gear. The pedals are directly connected to the rear wheel so if you stop pedalling, the bike will stop moving.

Freehub Mechanism in the rear hub which allows the wheel to coast when not being pedalled.

Full-suspension Term given to mountain bikes with front and rear suspension.

Go-Ride British Cycling's Club Development Programme aimed at improving both young riders and clubs.

Great Britain Cycling Team Professional, elite cycling team that represents Great Britain in national, international, Commonwealth and Olympic competition.

Hardtail Term given to a mountain bike with only front suspension.

Moto In BMX, a single-lap qualifying race.

National Cycle Network Network of cycle routes in the UK, created by the charity Sustrans.

Olympic Games Multi-sport event for all countries of the world. Cycling has been part of the Olympics since the first modern games in Athens in 1896. Mountain biking became an Olympic discipline in 1996 and BMX in 2008.

Paralympics Multi-sport event for athletes with physical, mental and sensorial disabilities. Cycling became part of the Paralympics in 1988.

Scottish Cycling National governing body for cyclesport in Scotland.

Stage race An on or off-road event over several days or even weeks with each day referred to as a stage.

Start gate Designated start position for certain track events, downhill mountain bike races, cycle speedway and BMX. Can be manual or automatically operated devices or as simple as a length of tape.

Time trial Individual or team event over set distance, against the clock.

UCI Union Cycliste Internationale. The association of national cycling federations, promoting cycling at an international level.

Velodrome Banked, oval track for cycle racing.

Welsh Cycling National governing body for cyclesport in Wales.

XC Commonly used abbreviation for cross-country mountain biking.

INDEX

USEFUL CONTACTS

British Cycling
www.britishcycling.org.uk

Cycling Ireland
www.cyclingireland.ie

Everyday Cycling
www.everydaycycling.com

Scottish Cycling
www.scuonline.org

Sustrans
www.sustrans.org.uk

Welsh Cycling
www.welshcycling.co.uk